Picture-Show by Siegfried Sassoon

Siegfried Loraine Sassoon was born on 8th September 1886.

Sassoon was educated at the New Beacon School, Sevenoaks, Kent then Marlborough College, Wiltshire and finally at Clare College, Cambridge, where from 1905 to 1907 he read history. He went down from Cambridge without a degree and spent the next few years indulging himself hunting, playing cricket and writing verse.

However, motivated by patriotism, Sassoon joined the Sussex Yeomanry of the British Army as the threat of war escalated into open conflict.

His early poems exhibit a Romantic, dilettantish sweetness but his war poetry moves to an increasingly discordant beat, stridently conveying the ugly truths of the trenches to an audience hitherto placated by jingoistic and patriotic propaganda.

Sassoon's periods of duty on the Western Front were marked by near-suicidal missions, including the single-handed capture of a German trench. Armed with grenades, he scattered sixty German soldiers.

In 1919 took up a post as literary editor of the socialist Daily Herald. Here he was responsible for employing several eminent reviewers, including E. M. Forster and Charlotte Mew. Sassoon also commissioned new material from the likes of Arnold Bennett and Osbert Sitwell.

Sassoon was now, in 1928, preparing to take a new direction by branching out into prose, with 'Memoirs of a Fox-Hunting Man'. This anonymously published first volume of a fictionalised autobiography, was acclaimed as a classic, bringing its author fame as a humorous writer. Other volumes including his own autobiography based on his youth and early manhood across three volumes followed.

In his last years Sassoon converted to Roman Catholicism and was admitted to the faith at Downside Abbey in Somerset.

Siegfried Loraine Sassoon, CBE, MC died from stomach cancer on 1st September 1967, a week before his 81st birthday.

Index of Contents

GW00686315

PICTURE-SHOW

And still they come and go: and this is all I know—
That from the gloom I watch an endless picture-show,
Where wild or listless faces flicker on their way,
With glad or grievous hearts I'll never understand
Because Time spins so fast, and they've no time to stay
Beyond the moment's gesture of a lifted hand.

And still, between the shadow and the blinding flame,
The brave despair of men flings onward, ever the same

As in those doom-lit years that wait them, and have been...
And life is just the picture dancing on a screen.

RECONCILIATION

When you are standing at your hero's grave,
Or near some homeless village where he died,
Remember, through your heart's rekindling pride,
The German soldiers who were loyal and brave.

Men fought like brutes; and hideous things were done;
And you have nourished hatred, harsh and blind.
But in that Golgotha perhaps you'll find
The mothers of the men who killed your son.

November, 1918.

CONCERT PARTY

(EGYPTIAN BASE CAMP)

They are gathering round...
Out of the twilight; over the grey-blue sand,
Shoals of low-jargoning men drift inward to the sound—
The jangle and throb of a piano ... tum-ti-tum...
Drawn by a lamp, they come
Out of the glimmering lines of their tents, over the shuffling sand.

O sing us the songs, the songs of our own land,
You warbling ladies in white.
Dimness conceals the hunger in our faces,
This wall of faces risen out of the night,
These eyes that keep their memories of the places
So long beyond their sight.

Jaded and gay, the ladies sing; and the chap in brown
Tilts his grey hat; jaunty and lean and pale,
He rattles the keys.... Some actor-bloke from town...
God send you home; and then A long, long trail;
I hear you calling me; and Dixieland....
Sing slowly ... now the chorus ... one by one
We hear them, drink them; till the concert's done.
Silent, I watch the shadowy mass of soldiers stand.
Silent, they drift away, over the glimmering sand.

KANTARA. April, 1918.

NIGHT ON THE CONVOY

(ALEXANDRIA-MARSEILLES)

Out in the blustering darkness, on the deck
A gleam of stars looks down. Long blurs of black,
The lean Destroyers, level with our track,
Plunging and stealing, watch the perilous way
Through backward racing seas and caverns of chill spray.
One sentry by the davits, in the gloom
Stands mute: the boat heaves onward through the night.
Shrouded is every chink of cabined light:
And sluiced by floundering waves that hiss and boom
And crash like guns, the troop-ship shudders ... doom.

Now something at my feet stirs with a sigh;
And slowly growing used to groping dark,
I know that the hurricane-deck, down all its length,
Is heaped and spread with lads in sprawling strength—
Blanketed soldiers sleeping. In the stark
Danger of life at war, they lie so still,
All prostrate and defenceless, head by head...
And I remember Arras, and that hill
Where dumb with pain I stumbled among the dead.

We are going home. The troopship, in a thrill
Of fiery-chamber'd anguish, throbs and rolls.
We are going home ... victims ... three thousand souls.

May, 1918.

THE DUG-OUT

Why do you lie with your legs ungainly huddled,
And one arm bent across your sullen, cold,
Exhausted face? It hurts my heart to watch you,
Deep-shadow'd from the candle's guttering gold;
And you wonder why I shake you by the shoulder;
Drowsy, you mumble and sigh and turn your head....

You are too young to fall asleep for ever;

And when you sleep you remind me of the dead.

ST. VENANT.
July, 1918.

BATTALION-RELIEF

'Fall in! Now get a move on.' (Curse the rain.)
We splash away along the straggling village,
Out to the flat rich country, green with June....
And sunset flares across wet crops and tillage,
Blazing with splendour-patches. (Harvest soon,
Up in the Line.) 'Perhaps the War'll be done
'By Christmas-Day. Keep smiling then, old son.'

Here's the Canal: it's dusk; we cross the bridge.
'Lead on there, by platoons.' (The Line's a-glare
With shellfire through the poplars; distant rattle
Of rifles and machine-guns.) 'Fritz is there!
'Christ, ain't it lively, Sergeant? Is't a battle?'
More rain: the lightning blinks, and thunder rumbles.
'There's over-head artillery!' some chap grumbles.

What's all this mob at the cross-roads? Where are the guides?...
'Lead on with number One.' And off they go.
'Three minute intervals.' (Poor blundering files,
Sweating and blindly burdened; who's to know
If death will catch them in those two dark miles?)
More rain. 'Lead on, Head-quarters.' (That's the lot.)

'Who's that? ... Oh, Sergeant-Major, don't get shot!
'And tell me, have we won this war or not!'

IN AN UNDERGROUND DRESSING-STATION

Quietly they set their burden down: he tried
To grin; moaned; moved his head from side to side.

He gripped the stretcher; stiffened; glared; and screamed,

'O put my leg down, doctor, do!' (He'd got
A bullet in his ankle; and he'd been shot
Horribly through the guts.) The surgeon seemed
So kind and gentle, saying, above that crying,

'You must keep still, my lad.' But he was dying.

I STOOD WITH THE DEAD

I stood with the Dead, so forsaken and still:
When dawn was grey I stood with the Dead.
And my slow heart said, 'You must kill, you must kill:
'Soldier, soldier, morning is red.'

On the shapes of the slain in their crumpled disgrace,
I stared for a while through the thin cold rain....
'O lad that I loved, there is rain on your face,
'And your eyes are blurred and sick like the plain.'

I stood with the Dead.... They were dead; they were dead;
My heart and my head beat a march of dismay:
And gusts of the wind came dulled by the guns.
'Fall in!' I shouted; 'Fall in for your pay!'

MEMORIAL TABLET

(GREAT WAR)

Squire nagged and bullied till I went to fight,
(Under Lord Derby's Scheme). I died in hell—
(They called it Passchendaele). My wound was slight,
And I was hobbling back; and then a shell
Burst slick upon the duck-boards: so I fell
Into the bottomless mud, and lost the light.

At sermon-time, while Squire is in his pew,
He gives my gilded name a thoughtful stare;
For, though low down upon the list, I'm there;
'In proud and glorious memory' ... that's my due.
Two bleeding years I fought in France, for Squire:
I suffered anguish that he's never guessed.
Once I came home on leave: and then went west...
What greater glory could a man desire?

ATROCITIES

You told me, in your drunken-boasting mood,

How once you butchered prisoners. That was good!
I'm sure you felt no pity while they stood
Patient and cowed and scared, as prisoners should.

How did you do them in? Come, don't be shy:
You know I love to hear how Germans die,
Downstairs in dug-outs. 'Kamerad!' They cry;
Then squeal like stoats when bombs begin to fly.

And you? I know your record. You went sick
When orders looked unwholesome: then, with trick
And lie, you wangled home. And here you are,
Still talking big and boozing in a bar.

TO LEONIDE MASSINE

IN 'CLEOPATRA'

O beauty doomed and perfect for an hour,
Leaping along the verge of death and night,
You show me dauntless Youth that went to fight
Four long years past, discovering pride and power.

You die but in our dreams, who watch you fall
Knowing that to-morrow you will dance again.
But not to ebbing music were they slain
Who sleep in ruined graves, beyond recall;
Who, following phantom-glory, friend and foe,
Into the darkness that was War must go;
Blind; banished from desire.
O mortal heart
Be still; you have drained the cup; you have played your part.

MEMORY

When I was young my heart and head were light,
And I was gay and feckless as a colt
Out in the fields, with morning in the may,
Wind on the grass, wings in the orchard bloom.
O thrilling sweet, my joy, when life was free,
And all the paths led on from hawthorn-time
Across the carolling meadows into June.

But now my heart is heavy-laden. I sit

Burning my dreams away beside the fire:
For death has made me wise and bitter and strong;
And I am rich in all that I have lost.
O starshine on the fields of long-ago,
Bring me the darkness and the nightingale;
Dim wealds of vanished summer, peace of home,
And silence; and the faces of my friends.

TO A VERY WISE MAN

I

Fires in the dark you build; tall quivering flames
In the huge midnight forest of the unknown.
Your soul is full of cities with dead names,
And blind-faced, earth-bound gods of bronze and stone
Whose priests and kings and lust-begotten lords
Watch the procession of their thundering hosts,
Or guard relentless fanes with flickering swords
And wizardry of ghosts.

II

In a strange house I woke; heard overhead
Hastily-thudding feet and a muffled scream...
(Is death like that?) ... I quaked uncomforted,
Striving to frame to-morrow in a dream
Of woods and sliding pools and cloudless day.
(You know how bees come into a twilight room
From dazzling afternoon, then sail away
Out of the curtained gloom.)

III

You understand my thoughts; though, when you think,
You're out beyond the boundaries of my brain.
I'm but a bird at dawn that cries, 'chink, chink'—
A garden-bird that warbles in the rain.
And you're the flying-man, the speck that steers
A careful course; far down the verge of day,
Half-way across the world. Above the years
You soar ... Is death so bad? ... I wish you'd say.

EARLY CHRONOLOGY

Slowly the daylight left our listening faces.
Professor Brown, with level baritone,
Discoursed into the dusk.
Five thousand years

He guided us through scientific spaces
Of excavated History, till the lone
Roads of research grew blurred, and in our ears
Time was the rumoured tongues of vanished races,
And Thought a chartless Age of Ice and Stone.

The story ended. Then the darkened air
Flowered as he lit his pipe; an aureole glowed
Enwreathed with smoke; the moment's match-light showed
His rosy face, broad brow, and smooth grey hair,
Backed by the crowded book-shelves.
In his wake

An archæologist began to make
Assumptions about aqueducts; (he quoted
Professor Sandstorm's book;) and soon they floated
Through desiccated forests; mangled myths;
And argued easily round megaliths.

Beyond the college garden something glinted:
A copper moon climbed clear above the trees.
Some Lydian coin? ... Professor Brown agrees
That copper coins were in that culture minted.
But, as her whitening way aloft she took,
I thought she had a pre-dynastic look.

ELEGY

(TO ROBERT ROSS)

Your dextrous wit will haunt us long
Wounding our grief with yesterday.
Your laughter is a broken song;
And death has found you, kind and gay.

We may forget those transient things
That made your charm and our delight:
But loyal love has deathless wings

That rise and triumph out of night.

So, in the days to come, your name
Shall be as music that ascends
When honour turns a heart from shame...
O heart of hearts! ... O friend of friends!

MIRACLES

I dreamt I saw a huge grey boat in silence steaming
Down a canal; it drew the dizzy landscape after;
The solemn world was sucked along with it—a streaming
Land-slide of loveliness. O, but I rocked with laughter,
Staring, and clinging to my tree-top. For a lake
Of gleaming peace swept on behind. (I mustn't wake.)

And then great clouds gathered and burst in spumes of green
That plunged into the water; and the sun came out
On glittering islands thronged with orchards scarlet-bloomed;
And rosy-plumed flamingoes flashed across the scene...
O, but the beauty of their freedom made me shout...
And when I woke I wondered where on earth I'd been.

THE GOLDSMITH

'This job's the best I've done.' He bent his head
Over the golden vessel that he'd wrought.
A bird was singing. But the craftsman's thought
Is a forgotten language, lost and dead.

He sigh'd and stretch'd brown arms. His friend came in
And stood beside him in the morning sun.
The goldwork glitter'd.... 'That's the best I've done.
'And now I've got a necklace to begin.'

This was at Gnossos, in the isle of Crete...
A girl was selling flowers along the street.

DEVOTION TO DUTY

I was near the King that day. I saw him snatch
And briskly scan the G.H.Q. dispatch.

Thick-voiced, he read it out. (His face was grave.)
'This officer advanced with the first wave,
'And when our first objective had been gained,
'(Though wounded twice), reorganized the line:
'The spirit of the troops was by his fine
'Example most effectively sustained.'

He gripped his beard; then closed his eyes and said,
'Bathsheba must be warned that he is dead.
'Send for her. I will be the first to tell
'This wife how her heroic husband fell.'

ANCIENT HISTORY

Adam, a brown old vulture in the rain,
Shivered below his wind-whipped olive-trees;
Huddling sharp chin on scarred and scraggy knees,
He moaned and mumbled to his darkening brain;
'He was the grandest of them all—was Cain!
'A lion laired in the hills, that none could tire;
'Swift as a stag; a stallion of the plain,
'Hungry and fierce with deeds of huge desire.'

Grimly he thought of Abel, soft and fair—
A lover with disaster in his face,
And scarlet blossom twisted in bright hair.
'Afraid to fight; was murder more disgrace? ...
'God always hated Cain.' ... He bowed his head—
The gaunt wild man whose lovely sons were dead.

SPORTING ACQUAINTANCES

I watched old squatting Chimpanzee: he traced
His painful patterns in the dirt: I saw
Red-haired Ourang-Utang, whimsical-faced,
Chewing a sportsman's meditative straw.
I'd met them years ago, and half-forgotten
They'd come to grief. (But how, I'd never heard,
Poor beggars!) Still, it seemed so rude and rotten
To stand and gape at them with never a word.

I ventured 'Ages since we met,' and tried
My candid smile of friendship. No success.
One scratched his hairy thigh, while t'other sighed

And glanced away. I saw they liked me less
Than when, on Epsom Downs, in cloudless weather,
We backed The Tetrarch and got drunk together.

WHAT THE CAPTAIN SAID AT THE POINT-TO-POINT

I've had a good bump round; my little horse
Refused the brook first time,
Then jumped it prime;
And ran out at the double,
But of course
There's always trouble at a double:
And then—I don't know how
It was—he turned it up
At that big, hairy fence before the plough;
And some young silly pup,
(I don't know which),
Near as a toucher knocked me into the ditch;
But we finished full of running, and quite sound:
And anyhow I've had a good bump round.

CINEMA HERO

O, this is more than fiction! It's the truth
That somehow never happened. Pay your bob,
And walk straight in, abandoning To-day.
(To-day's a place outside the picture-house;
Forget it, and the film will do the rest.)

There's nothing fine in being as large as life:
The splendour starts when things begin to move
And gestures grow enormous. That's the way
To dramatise your dreams and play the part
As you'd have done if luck had starred your face.

I'm 'Rupert from the Mountains'! (Pass the stout)...
Yes, I'm the Broncho Boy we watched to-night,
That robbed a ranch and galloped down the creek.
(Moonlight and shattering hoofs.... O moonlight of the West!
Wind in the gum-trees, and my swerving mare
Beating her flickering shadow on the post.)
Ah, I was wild in those fierce days! You saw me
Fix that saloon? They stared into my face
And slowly put their hands up, while I stood

With dancing eyes,—romantic to the world!

Things happened afterwards ... You know the story...
The sheriff's daughter, bandaging my head;
Love at first sight; the escape; and making good
(To music by Mascagni). And at last—
Peace; and the gradual beauty of my smile.

But that's all finished now. One has to take
Life as it comes. I've nothing to regret.
For men like me, the only thing that counts
Is the adventure. Lord, what times I've had!

God and King Charles! And then my mistress's arms....
(To-morrow evening I'm a Cavalier.)

Well, what's the news to-night about the Strike?

FANCY DRESS

Some Brave, awake in you to-night,
Knocked at your heart: an eagle's flight
Stirred in the feather on your head.
Your wide-set Indian eyes, alight
Above high cheek-bones smeared with red,
Unveiled cragg'd centuries, and led
You, the snared wraith of bygone things—
Wild ancestries of trackless Kings—
Out of the past.... So men have felt
Strange anger move them as they knelt
Praying to gods serenely starred
In heavens where tomahawks are barred.

MIDDLE-AGES

I heard a clash, and a cry,
And a horseman fleeing the wood.
The moon hid in a cloud.
Deep in shadow I stood.
'Ugly work!' thought I,
Holding my breath.
'Men must be cruel and proud,
'Jousting for death.'

With gusty glimmering shone
The moon; and the wind blew colder.
A man went over the hill,
Bent to his horse's shoulder.
'Time for me to be gone'...
Darkly I fled.
Owls in the wood were shrill,
And the moon sank red.

THE PORTRAIT

I watch you, gazing at me from the wall,
And wonder how you'd match your dreams with mine,
If, mastering time's illusion, I could call
You back to share this quiet candle-shine.

For you were young, three-hundred years ago;
And by your looks I guess that you were wise...
Come, whisper soft, and Death will never know
You've slipped away from those calm, painted eyes.

Strange is your voice ... Poor ninny, dead so long,
And all your pride forgotten like your name.
'One April morn I heard a blackbird's song,
'And joy was in my heart like leaves aflame.'

And so you died before your songs took wing;
While Andrew Marvell followed in your wake.
'Love thrilled me into music. I could sing
But for a moment,—but for beauty's sake.'

Who passes? There's a star-lit breeze that stirs
The glimmer of white lilies in the gloom.
Who speaks? Death has his silent messengers:
And there was more than silence in this room

While you were gazing at me from the wall
And wondering how you'd match your dreams with mine,
If, mastering time's illusion, you could call
Me back to share your vanished candle-shine.

BUTTERFLIES

Frail travellers, deftly flickering over the flowers;

O living flowers against the heedless blue
Of summer days, what sends them dancing through
This fiery-blossom'd revel of the hours?

Theirs are the musing silences between
The enraptured crying of shrill birds that make
Heaven in the wood while summer dawns awake;
And theirs the faintest winds that hush the green.

And they are as my soul that wings its way
Out of the starlit dimness into morn:
And they are as my tremulous being—born
To know but this, the phantom glare of day.

WRAITHS

They know not the green leaves;
In whose earth-haunting dream
Dimly the forest heaves,
And voiceless goes the stream.
Strangely they seek a place
In love's night-memoried hall;
Peering from face to face,
Until some heart shall call
And keep them, for a breath,
Half-mortal ... (Hark to the rain!) ...
They are dead ... (O hear how death
Gropes on the shutter'd pane!)

PHANTOM

The clock has stopped; and the wind's dropped:
A candle burns with moon-gold flame.
Blank silence whispers at my ears,
'Though I've been dead these coffin'd years,
'You'll never choke my shame.'

'Dip your quill in clotted ink:
'Write; I'll quicken you to think
'In my old fiery alphabet.'
The candle-flame upon its wick
Staggers; the time-piece starts to tick;
And down the dark the wind blows wet.

Good angels, help me to forget.

THE DARK HOUSE

Dusk in the rain-soaked garden,
And dark the house within.
A door creaked: someone was early
To watch the dawn begin.
But he stole away like a thief
In the chilly, star-bright air:
Though the house was shuttered for slumber,
He had left one wakeful there.

Nothing moved in the garden.
Never a bird would sing,
Nor shake and scatter the dew from the boughs
With shy and startled wing.
But when that lover had passed the gate
A quavering thrush began...
'Come back; come back!' he shrilled to the heart
Of the passion-plighted man.

IDYLL

In the grey summer garden I shall find you
With day-break and the morning hills behind you.
There will be rain-wet roses; stir of wings;
And down the wood a thrush that wakes and sings.
Not from the past you'll come, but from that deep
Where beauty murmurs to the soul asleep:
And I shall know the sense of life re-born
From dreams into the mystery of morn
Where gloom and brightness meet. And standing there
Till that calm song is done, at last we'll share
The league-spread, quiring symphonies that are
Joy in the world, and peace, and dawn's one star.

PARTED

Sleepless I listen to the surge and drone
And drifting roar of the town's undertone;
Till through quiet falling rain I hear the bells

Tolling and chiming their brief tune that tells
Day's midnight end. And from the day that's over
No flashes of delight I can recover;
But only dreary winter streets, and faces
Of people moving in loud clanging places:
And I in my loneliness, longing for you...

For all I did to-day, and all I'll do
To-morrow, in this city of intense
Arteried activities that throb and strive,
Is but a beating down of that suspense
Which holds me from your arms.
I am alive
Only that I may find you at the end
Of these slow-striking hours I toil to spend,
Putting each one behind me, knowing but this—
That all my days are turning toward your kiss;
That all expectancy awaits the deep
Consoling passion of your eyes, that keep
Their radiance for my coming, and their peace
For when I find in you my love's release.

LOVERS

You were glad to-night: and now you've gone away.
Flushed in the dark, you put your dreams to bed;
But as you fall asleep I hear you say
Those tired sweet drowsy words we left unsaid.

I am alone: but in the windless night
I listen to the gurgling rain that veils
The gloom with peace; and whispering of your white
Limbs, and your mouth that stormed my throat with bliss,
The rain becomes your voice, and tells me tales
That crowd my heart with memories of your kiss.

Sleep well: for I can follow you, to bless
And lull your distant beauty where you roam;
And with wild songs of hoarded loveliness
Recall you to these arms that were your home.

SLUMBER-SONG

Sleep; and my song shall build about your bed

A Paradise of dimness. You shall feel
The folding of tired wings; and peace will dwell
Throned in your silence: and one hour shall hold
Summer, and midnight, and immensity
Lulled to forgetfulness. For, where you dream,
The stately gloom of foliage shall embower
Your slumbering thought with tapestries of blue.
And there shall be no memory of the sky,
Nor sunlight with its cruelty of swords.
But, to your soul that sinks from deep to deep
Through drowned and glimmering colour, Time shall be
Only slow rhythmic swaying; and your breath;
And roses in the darkness; and my love.

THE IMPERFECT LOVER

I never asked you to be perfect—did I?—
Though often I've called you sweet, in the invasion
Of mastering love. I never prayed that you
Might stand, unsoiled, angelic and inhuman,
Pointing the way toward Sainthood like a sign-post.

Oh yes, I know the way to heaven was easy.
We found the little kingdom of our passion
That all can share who walk the road of lovers.
In wild and secret happiness we stumbled;
And gods and demons clamoured in our senses.

But I've grown thoughtful now. And you have lost
Your early-morning freshness of surprise
At being so utterly mine: you've learned to fear
The gloomy, stricken places in my soul,
And the occasional ghosts that haunt my gaze.

You made me glad; and I can still return
To you, the haven of my lonely pride:
But I am sworn to murder those illusions
That blossom from desire with desperate beauty:
And there shall be no falsehood in our failure;
Since, if we loved like beasts, the thing is done,
And I'll not hide it, though our heaven be hell.

You dream long liturgies of our devotion.
Yet, in my heart, I dread our love's destruction.
But, should you grow to hate me, I would ask
No mercy of your mood: I'd have you stand

And look me in the eyes, and laugh, and smite me.

Then I should know, at least, that truth endured,
Though love had died of wounds. And you could leave me
Unvanquished in my atmosphere of devils.

VISION

I love all things that pass: their briefness is
Music that fades on transient silences.
Winds, birds, and glittering leaves that flare and fall—
They fling delight across the world; they call
To rhythmic-flashing limbs that rove and race...
A moment in the dawn for Youth's lit face;
A moment's passion, closing on the cry—
'O Beauty, born of lovely things that die!'

TO A CHILDLESS WOMAN

You think I cannot understand. Ah, but I do ...
I have been wrung with anger and compassion for you.
I wonder if you'd loathe my pity, if you knew.

But you shall know. I've carried in my heart too long
This secret burden. Has not silence wrought your wrong—
Brought you to dumb and wintry middle-age, with grey
Unfruitful withering?—Ah, the pitiless things I say...

What do you ask your God for, at the end of day,
Kneeling beside your bed with bowed and hopeless head?
What mercy can He give you?—Dreams of the unborn
Children that haunt your soul like loving words unsaid—
Dreams, as a song half-heard through sleep in early morn?

I see you in the chapel, where you bend before
The enhaloed calm of everlasting Motherhood
That wounds your life; I see you humbled to adore
The painted miracle you've never understood.
Tender, and bitter-sweet, and shy, I've watched you holding
Another's child. O childless woman, was it then
That, with an instant's cry, your heart, made young again,
Was crucified for ever—those poor arms enfolding
The life, the consummation that had been denied you?
I too have longed for children. Ah, but you must not weep.

Something I have to whisper as I kneel beside you...
And you must pray for me before you fall asleep.

AFTERMATH

Have you forgotten yet? ...
For the world's events have rumbled on since those gagged days,
Like traffic checked awhile at the crossing of city-ways:
And the haunted gap in your mind has filled with thoughts that flow
Like clouds in the lit heavens of life; and you're a man reprieved to go,
Taking your peaceful share of Time, with joy to spare.
But the past is just the same—and War's a bloody game...
Have you forgotten yet? ...
Look down, and swear by the slain of the War that
you'll never forget.

Do you remember the dark months you held the sector at Mametz—
The nights you watched and wired and dug and piled sandbags on parapets?
Do you remember the rats; and the stench
Of corpses rotting in front of the front-line trench—
And dawn coming, dirty-white, and chill with a hopeless rain?
Do you ever stop and ask, 'Is it all going to happen again?'

Do you remember that hour of din before the attack—
And the anger, the blind compassion that seized and shook you then
As you peered at the doomed and haggard faces of your men?
Do you remember the stretcher-cases lurching back
With dying eyes and lolling heads—those ashen-grey
Masks of the lads who once were keen and kind and gay?

Have you forgotten yet? ...
Look up, and swear by the green of the spring that you'll never forget.

March, 1919.

FALLING ASLEEP

Voices moving about in the quiet house:
Thud of feet and a muffled shutting of doors:
Everyone yawning ... only the clocks are alert.

Out in the night there's autumn-smelling gloom
Crowded with whispering trees,—looming of oaks
That roared in wild wet gales: across the park

The hollow cry of hounds like lonely bells:
And I know that the clouds are moving across the moon,
The low, red, rising moon.
The herons call
And wrangle by their pool; and hooting owls
Sail from the wood across pale stocks of wheat.

Waiting for sleep, I drift from thoughts like these;
And where to-day was dream-like, build my dreams.
Music ... there was a bright white room below,
And someone singing a song about a soldier,—
One hour, two hours ago; and soon the song
Will be 'last night': but now the beauty swings
Across my brain, ghost of remember'd chords
Which still can make such radiance in my dream
That I can watch the marching of my soldiers,
And count their faces; faces; sunlit faces.

Falling asleep ... the herons, and the hounds...
September in the darkness; and the world
I've known; all fading past me into peace.

PRELUDE TO AN UNWRITTEN MASTERPIECE

You like my bird-sung gardens: wings and flowers;
Calm landscapes for emotion; star-lit lawns;
And Youth against the sun-rise ... 'Not profound;
'But such a haunting music in the sound:
'Do it once more; it helps us to forget.'

Last night I dreamt an old recurring scene—
Some complex out of childhood; (sex, of course!)
I can't remember how the trouble starts;
And then I'm running blindly in the sun
Down the old orchard, and there's something cruel
Chasing me; someone roused to a grim pursuit
Of clumsy anger ... Crash! I'm through the fence
And thrusting wildly down the wood that's dense
With woven green of safety; paths that wind
Moss-grown from glade to glade; and far behind,
One thwarted yell; then silence. I've escaped.

That's where it used to stop. Last night I went
Onward until the trees were dark and huge,
And I was lost, cut off from all return
By swamps and birdless jungles. I'd no chance

Of getting home for tea. I woke with shivers,
And thought of crocodiles in crawling rivers.

Some day I'll build (more ruggedly than Doughty)
A dark tremendous song you'll never hear.
My beard will be a snow-storm, drifting whiter
On bowed, prophetic shoulders, year by year.
And some will say, 'His work has grown so dreary.'
Others, 'He used to be a charming writer.'
And you, my friend, will query—
'Why can't you cut it short, you pompous blighter?'

LIMITATIONS

If you could crowd them into forty lines!
Yes; you can do it, once you get a start:
All that you want is waiting in your head,
For long-ago you've learnt it off by heart.

Begin: your mind's the room where you must sleep,
(Don't pause for rhymes), till twilight wakes you early.
The window stands wide-open, as it stood
When tree-tops loomed enchanted for a child
Hearing the dawn's first thrushes through the wood
Warbling (you know the words) serene and wild.

You've said it all before: you dreamed of Death,
A dim Apollo in the bird-voiced breeze
That drifts across the morning veiled with showers,
While golden weather shines among dark trees.

You've got your limitations; let them sing,
And all your life will waken with a cry:
Why should you halt when rapture's on the wing
And you've no limit but the cloud-flocked sky?...

But some chap shouts, 'Here, stop it; that's been done!'—
As God might holloa to the rising sun,
And then relent, because the glorying rays
Reminded Him of glinting Eden days,
And Adam's trustful eyes as he looks up
From carving eagles on his beechwood cup.

Young Adam knew his job; he could condense
Life to an eagle from the unknown immense ...
Go on, whoever you are; your lines can be

A whisper in the music from the weirs
Of song that plunge and tumble toward the sea
That is the uncharted mercy of our tears.

I told you it was easy: words are fools
Who follow blindly, once they get a lead.
But thoughts are kingfishers that haunt the pools
Of quiet; seldom-seen; and all you need
Is just that flash of joy above your dream.
So, when those forty platitudes are done,
You'll hear a bird-note calling from the stream
That wandered through your childhood; and the sun
Will strike the old flaming wonder from the waters ...
And there'll be forty lines not yet begun.

EVERYONE SANG

Everyone suddenly burst out singing;
And I was filled with such delight
As prisoned birds must find in freedom,
Winging wildly across the white
Orchards and dark-green fields; on—on—and out of sight.

Everyone's voice was suddenly lifted;
And beauty came like the setting sun:
My heart was shaken with tears; and horror
Drifted away ... O, but Everyone
Was a bird; and the song was wordless; the singing will never be done.

Siegfried Sassoon – A Short Biography

Siegfried Loraine Sassoon was born on 8th September 1886. He grew up in the neo-gothic mansion 'Weirleigh', in Matfield, Kent.

His father, Alfred Ezra Sassoon, was a member of the wealthy Baghdadi Jewish Sassoon merchant family. For marrying outside the faith he was disinherited. His mother, Theresa, was from the Anglo-Catholic Thornycroft family, the sculptors responsible for many of the best-known statues in London. Interestingly she named him Siegfried because of her love for Wagner's operas rather than any German ancestry. He was the second of three sons. When he was four years old his parents separated.

Sassoon was educated at the New Beacon School, Sevenoaks, Kent then Marlborough College, Wiltshire and finally at Clare College, Cambridge, where from 1905 to 1907 he read history. He went down from Cambridge without a degree and spent the next few years indulging himself hunting, playing cricket and writing verse: some of which he published privately. Sassoon had only a small private income that, provided he lived modestly, negated the need to work, though in later years he would be left a generous legacy by his aunt, Rachel Beer, allowing him to buy the estate of Heytesbury House in Wiltshire.

His first published success, 'The Daffodil Murderer' (1913), was a parody of John Masefield's 'The Everlasting Mercy'. His great friend Robert Graves describes it as a "parody of Masefield which, midway through, had forgotten to be a parody and turned into rather good Masefield."

Sassoon was a good amateur cricketer and was keen to play for Kent County Cricket Club. He often turned out for the Bluemantles, where he sometimes played alongside another keen cricketer, Arthur Conan Doyle. Although an enthusiast, Sassoon was not good enough to play for Kent, but he continued to play cricket into his seventies.

Sassoon had proffered his opinions on the political situation before the First World War thus—"France was a lady, Russia was a bear, and performing in the county cricket team was much more important than either of them".

However, motivated by patriotism, Sassoon joined the British Army as the threat of war escalated. He was in service with the Sussex Yeomanry on 4th August 1914, the day war was declared on Germany.

He broke his arm badly in a riding accident and was therefore out of action before even leaving England. He spent the spring of 1915 convalescing. Sassoon was commissioned into the 3rd Battalion (Special Reserve), Royal Welch Fusiliers, as a second lieutenant on 29th May 1915. On 1st November his younger brother Hamo was killed in the Gallipoli Campaign, and that same month Sassoon was sent to the 1st Battalion in France. There he met Robert Graves, and they became close friends, drawn together by their poetic ambitions, they would read and discuss each other's work. Graves' views on what may be called 'gritty realism' profoundly affected Sassoon's idea of what poetry was. Life on the front line meant he soon became horrified by the slaughter and daily realities of war, and the tone of his writing changed dramatically: where his early poems exhibit a Romantic, dilettantish sweetness, his war poetry moves to an increasingly discordant beat, stridently conveying the ugly truths of the trenches to an audience hitherto placated by jingoistic and patriotic propaganda.

Conversely Sassoon's periods of duty on the Western Front were marked by exceptionally brave actions, including the single-handed capture of a German trench in the Hindenburg Line. Armed with grenades, he scattered sixty German soldiers.

Sassoon's bravery was so inspiring that his fellow soldiers said they felt confident only when they were accompanied by him. He often went out on night-raids and bombing patrols and demonstrated ruthless efficiency as a company commander. Deepening depression at the horror and misery the soldiers were forced to endure produced in Sassoon a paradoxically manic courage, and earned him the nickname 'Mad Jack' by his men for his many and near-suicidal exploits. On 27th July 1916 Sassoon was awarded the Military Cross. He was also later recommended for the Victoria Cross.

His poetry both described the horrors of the trenches and satirised the patriotic pretensions of those who, in Sassoon's view, were responsible for a jingoism-fuelled war.

Despite his decorations and reputation, in 1917 Sassoon decided to make a stand against the running of the war. At the end of a spell of convalescent leave, Sassoon declined to return to duty; instead, encouraged by pacifist friends such as Bertrand Russell and Lady Ottoline Morrell, he sent a letter to his commanding officer entitled 'Finished with the War: A Soldier's Declaration'. Forwarded to the press and read out in the House of Commons by a sympathetic member of Parliament, the letter was seen by some as treasonous ('I am making this statement as an act of wilful defiance of military authority') and by others as condemning the war government's motives ('I believe that the war upon which I entered as a war of defence and liberation has now become a war of aggression and conquest'). Rather than court-martial Sassoon, the authorities decided that he was unfit for service and had him sent to Craiglockhart War Hospital near Edinburgh. This facility had opened in 1916 as a military psychiatric hospital to care for officers suffering from the psychological effects of the Great War, such as neurasthenia ('shell shock').

At Craiglockhart, Sassoon met Wilfred Owen, a poet who would eventually exceed him in fame. It was perhaps thanks to Sassoon that Owen persevered in his ambition to write better poetry. Both men returned to active service in France. Owen would later be killed in 1918, just a week before Armistice. Sassoon, despite all this, was promoted to lieutenant, and having spent some time away from danger in Palestine, eventually returned to the front line.

On 13th July 1918, Sassoon was almost immediately wounded again—by friendly fire when he was shot in the head by a British soldier who had mistaken him for a German near Arras, France. As a result, he spent the remaining months of the war in Britain. By this time he had been promoted to acting captain.

On 12th March 1919 Sassoon relinquished his commission on health grounds but was allowed to retain the rank of captain.

He now dabbled briefly in the politics of the Labour movement which was now gathering strength after the first two tumultuous decades of the 20th Century.

In 1919 took up a post as literary editor of the socialist Daily Herald. Here he was responsible for employing several eminent names as reviewers, including E. M. Forster and Charlotte Mew. Sassoon also commissioned new material from the likes of Arnold Bennett and Osbert Sitwell. He also managed to now extend his own interests to include music.

Sassoon now accepted a lecture tour of the United States and travelled throughout Europe and across Britain. He came into possession of a car, a gift from the publisher Frankie Schuster. He became renowned among his friends for his poor driving skills, which apparently did not discourage him from making full use of the car.

In 1923 he visited Wales. Sassoon was a great admirer of the Welsh poet Henry Vaughan and paid a pilgrimage to his grave at Llansantffraed, Powys. It was there he wrote one of his best-known peacetime poems, 'At the Grave of Henry Vaughan'.

Unhappily there came the deaths in quick succession of three of his closest friends; Edmund Gosse, Thomas Hardy and Frankie Schuster, causing a serious setback to his personal happiness.

Sassoon was now, in 1928, preparing to take a new direction by branching out into prose, with 'Memoirs of a Fox-Hunting Man'. This anonymously published first volume of a fictionalised autobiography, was acclaimed as a classic, bringing its author fame as a humorous writer. The book won the 1928 James Tait Black Award for fiction. Sassoon followed it with 'Memoirs of an Infantry Officer' (1930) and 'Sherston's Progress' (1936). Some time later he would write his own autobiography based on his youth and early manhood across three volumes, which were also widely acclaimed. These were 'The Old Century', 'The Weald of Youth' and 'Siegfried's Journey'.

Sassoon, having matured greatly as a result of his military service, continued to seek long-lasting, loving relationships. Initially these were with a succession of men.

In September 1931, Sassoon rented Fitz House, Teffont Magna, Wiltshire and began to live there. In December 1933, he married Hester Gatty, who was many years his junior. The marriage led to the birth of a child, George, which he had craved for a long time.

By 1945 Sassoon was separated from his wife and was living in seclusion at Heytesbury in Wiltshire, although he continued to keep contact with a circle which included E.M. Forster and J.R. Ackerley. One of his closest friends was the cricketer, Dennis Silk who would become Warden (headmaster) of Radley College. He also formed a close friendship with Vivien Hancock, the headmistress of Greenways School at Ashton Gifford, where his son George was a pupil. This provoked Hester to make strong accusations against her who then responded with a threat of legal action.

In his last years Sassoon converted to Roman Catholicism. He had hoped that Ronald Knox, a Roman Catholic priest and writer whom he admired, would instruct him in the faith, but Knox was too ill to take on the task. The priest Sebastian Moore was chosen to instruct him instead, and Sassoon was admitted to the faith at Downside Abbey in Somerset. He also paid regular visits to the nuns at Stanbrook Abbey, and their press printed commemorative editions of some of his poems.

Sassoon was appointed Commander of the Order of the British Empire (CBE) in the 1951 New Year Honours.

Siegfried Loraine Sassoon, CBE, MC died from stomach cancer on 1st September 1967, a week before his 81st birthday. He is buried at St Andrew's Church, Mells, Somerset.

On 11th November 1985, Sassoon was among sixteen Great War poets commemorated on a slate stone unveiled in Westminster Abbey's Poet's Corner. The inscription on the stone was written by friend and fellow War poet Wilfred Owen. It reads: "My subject is War, and the pity of War. The Poetry is in the pity."

Siegried Sassoon – A Concise Bibliography

Poetry
The Daffodil Murderer (1913)
The Old Huntsman and Other Poems (1917)
Counter-Attack and Other Poems (1918)
The War Poems of Siegfried Sassoon (1919)
Picture-Show (1919)
Recreations (1923)
Lingual Exercises for Advanced Vocabularians (1925)
Selected Poems (1925)
Satirical Poems (1926)

The Heart's Journey (1928)
Poems by Pinchbeck Lyre (1931)
The Road to Ruin (1933)
Vigils (1935)
Rhymed Ruminations (1940)
Poems Newly Selected (1940)
Collected Poems (1947)
Common Chords (1950/1951)
Emblems of Experience (1951)
The Tasking (1954)
Sequences (1956)
Lenten Illuminations (1959)
The Path to Peace (1960)
Collected Poems 1908-1956 (1961)
The War Poems ed. Rupert Hart-Davis (1983)

Prose

Memoirs of a Fox-Hunting Man (1928)
Memoirs of an Infantry Officer (1930)
Sherston's Progress (1936)
Complete Memoirs of George Sherston (1937)
The Old Century (1938)
On Poetry (1939)
The Weald of Youth (1942)
Siegfried's Journey (1945)
Meredith (1948)

Other Works

Finished with the War: A Soldier's Declaration (1917)
"Introduction" to Poems by Wilfred Owen (1920)